EXTREME SPORTS BIOGRAPHIES ™

TRAVIS PASTRANA
Motocross Champion

Ian F. Mahaney

The Rosen Publishing Group's
PowerKids Press ™
New York

To my wife, Jenet

Safety gear, including knee-high plastic boots, chest protectors, nylon pants, and a full-face helmet designed specifically for motocross, should be worn while riding motocross. Do not attempt tricks without proper gear, instruction, and supervision.

Published in 2005 by The Rosen Publishing Group, Inc.
29 East 21st Street, New York, NY 10010

First Edition

Editor: Heidi Leigh Johansen
Book Design: Mike Donnellan
Photo Researcher: Peter Tomlinson

Photo Credits: Cover, pp. 12, 22 © Larry Kasparek/NewSport/CORBIS; pp. 4, 8 (inset) Diane Moore/Icon SMI; p. 4 (inset) Shelly Castellano/Icon SMI; p. 7 (left) Royalty-Free/CORBIS; p. 7 (right) Tony Donaldson/Icon SMI; pp. 8, 11 Icon Sports Media; pp. 15, 16 © AP/Wide World Photos; p. 16 (inset) © Duomo/CORBIS; p. 19 Zuma Press; p. 20 © AP Photo/Elyria Chronicle Telegram, Haraz Ghanbari; p. 20 (inset) © Shazamm.

Library of Congress Cataloging-in-Publication Data

Mahaney, Ian F.
Travis Pastrana : motocross champion / Ian F. Mahaney.— 1st ed.
    p. cm. — (Extreme sports biographies)
ISBN 1-4042-2748-2 (Library Binding)
1. Pastrana, Travis, 1983—Juvenile literature. 2. Motorcyclists—United States—Biography—Juvenile literature. 3. Motocross—Juvenile literature. [1. Pastrana, Travis, 1983– 2. Motorcyclists. 3. Motocross.] I. Title. II. Series.

GV1060.2.P39M35 2005
796.72'092—dc22

                    2003026633

Manufactured in the United States of America

Contents

1 Extreme Motocross   5

2 Getting to Know Travis Pastrana   6

3 Travis Begins Racing   9

4 The Racer   10

5 The Trickster   13

6 Rookie of the Year   14

7 X-Games Champion   17

8 Travis's Cool Tricks   18

9 Safety First   21

10 A Smart Guy   22

Glossary   23

Index   24

Web Sites   24

Travis Pastrana races his motorcycle on a bumpy dirt course. You may hear the term "supercross." Supercross, which is short for the Super Bowl of motocross, is the name for indoor motocross. Inset: Travis smiles big after a race in California.

Extreme Motocross

An **extreme sport** is an **exciting** and daring sport. Skateboarding, wakeboarding, and motocross are examples of extreme sports. Motocross may be the most extreme of all extreme sports. In motocross, riders drive motorcycles, or motorized bikes, and **perform** tricks in the air. There are two main types of motocross. The first type is racing. In racing, riders speed around a dirt track that has jumps and other **obstacles**. The person who finishes a certain number of laps around the dirt course first is the winner of the race. The second type of motocross is called freeriding. In freeriding, motocross riders jump into the air and complete tricks using obstacles. Travis Pastrana is a well-known motocross racer and freerider. He is one of the most successful motocross **champions** of all time.

Getting to Know Travis Pastrana

Travis Pastrana was born on October 8, 1983, in Annapolis, Maryland. When Travis was four years old, his parents, Robert and Debby, gave him the best Christmas gift he could imagine. They gave Travis a small motorcycle. It was a one-speed motorcycle called a Honda Z-50. "One-speed" means that Travis did not have to change the gears while riding the motorcycle. Other motorcycles have gears that allow the motorcycles to go faster with each gear change. Today Travis rides motorcycles that have gears that he changes as he rides. "Z-50" is the name for the engine size of Travis's first motorcycle. A 50 cubic centimeter (cc) engine is very small. A motorcycle with an engine this size is simpler to ride than a motorcycle with a larger engine. Robert Pastrana showed Travis how to ride the motorcycle, or the bike as it is often called, near their home.

Motocross bikes come in many sizes. The main difference among them is the engine size. Above Left: Travis's first bike was small, like the bikes shown here. Above Right: Today Travis rides 125 cc and 250 cc motorcycles, which means that the engines of these bikes are 125 or 250 cubic centimeters.

Travis keeps an eye on the competition. His racing shirt is made by Suzuki, the name of the first company to sponsor him. His yellow motorcycle has sturdy parts and sides. Inset: Travis pulls a wide turn in an Anaheim, California race.

Travis Begins Racing

When Robert Pastrana taught Travis how to ride a motorcycle, Robert taught Travis properly. Robert showed Travis how to speed up, to turn, and to brake. Safety is very important on a motorcycle! Only after Travis practiced these basic lessons could he move on to more **difficult** moves on his motorcycle. Then Robert taught his son to race on the motorcycle. Travis entered his first motorcycle **competition** when he was eight years old. Travis competed in that race with a 50 cc motorcycle. Motocross races are **organized** by engine size. Travis competed against other boys racing motorcycles of the same size. Racing went so well for Travis that he was **sponsored** by American Suzuki, a well-known motorcycle company, when he was only eight years old! This means that Suzuki gave Travis free motorcycles and clothing and also paid for him to compete in motocross events.

Although Travis Pastrana entered his first race when he was eight, he did not see **professionals** race until he was 10 years old. Travis's parents took Travis to watch professionals race at a motocross track called Southwick. At Southwick, Travis saw some of the best professional riders in the country race one another on big 125 cc and 250 cc motorcycles. After this event Travis knew he wanted to race big motorcycles. Travis worked hard and learned new tricks. When Travis was 13, he entered his first 125 cc motorcycle race. Travis was having a fun time riding, and it certainly helped that he became successful very quickly. Travis won the National **Amateur** Championship five times between 1992 and 1999. In 1997 and 1999, when he was 14 and 16, Travis also won **medals** at amateur races called Loretta Lynn's Amateur National Championships in Tennessee.

Many motocross tricks, such as the big jump Travis performs here, can be unsafe. Travis's family and friends are very supportive of his love for motocross. They are very concerned about his safety, though.

Travis performs a backflip to win the gold medal in the 2002 Gravity Games Moto-X event. The Gravity Games is an extreme sports competition held every year in different locations. Motocross is often called Moto-X. This is because the letter X is made with two crossing lines, so X stands for "cross."

The Trickster

Travis Pastrana is a great racer. He is even better when it comes to performing tricks as a freerider. In freeriding, Travis performs tricks off jumps and obstacles. There are three main freeriding events. The first is called freestyle. In freestyle, bikers ride on a dirt course with jumps. The object in freestyle is to perform difficult tricks in the air off the jumps. The second event is called big air. The big air competition is an event in which riders jump into the air off a huge jump that is 20 feet (6 m) long. Some riders, including Travis, even do backflips in the big air event. This is a very **dangerous** event, because the bikers ride more than 50 feet (15 m) into the air off the jump. Step up is the final event. The object of the step up event is to jump over a **horizontal** pole. The bar is raised higher for each competitor who jumps over it. Travis can jump over a horizontal pole that is 30 feet (9 m) high!

Rookie of the Year

When Travis turned 16, he became a professional, or pro, motocross rider. This means that competing in motocross events became Travis's job. Travis earns money as a motocross racer while competing in the most exciting motocross events in the United States and in the world. Travis did very well in his **rookie** season in 2000, or his first year as a professional. Travis won events in St. Louis, Missouri, and Daytona Beach, Florida. Travis also won the American Motorcycle Association (AMA) National Championship in the 125 cc class, or the events in which riders rode 125 cc motorcycles. The AMA is a company that organizes motocross events around the country. That year Travis raced so successfully that he was voted Rookie of the Year by the AMA. In 2001, Travis was the AMA's eastern supercross champion.

Travis performs an unbelievable trick in which he rides his bike off a jump, flies through the air, and then does a midair handstand while holding on tight to the handlebars. He uses his body strength to swing back to his seat for his landing.

Travis pulls a daredevil jump, barely holding on to his bike with one hand, at the 2000 X Games. Travis won gold medals at the 2000 and 2001 X Games. Travis also won gold medals in 1999 and 2002 at the Gravity Games. Inset: Travis catches air in an X-Games competition.

X-Games Champion

The X Games is an extreme sports competition held every year in the winter and the summer. Motocross, skateboarding, and snowboarding are examples of X-Games events. Travis first competed in the motocross freestyle event at the X Games in 1999, when the X Games was held in San Francisco, California. Travis rode very well throughout the competition and then he performed a **daredevil** move at the end of his ride. He rode his bike off a **ramp** 100 feet (30.5 m) into the air. Then he went off course and he dove, with his bike, into San Francisco Bay. It was a very daring move but it was also a very dangerous and harmful one. Travis won many fans with this move, but he also made enemies. Many X-Games officials and San Francisco police officers were angry. Travis won first place in the freestyle event but was forced to use his prize money to clean up the bay.

Travis's Cool Tricks

Travis is best known for a trick called the Superman seat grab. In this trick, Travis jumps off a dirt ramp into the air. Then he kicks his legs off the bike and grabs the handlebars with one hand and the seat with the other hand. Sometimes he even lets go of the handlebars and holds his bike with only one hand. Travis holds his body **parallel** to the ground as the bike moves through the air, so that he looks like Superman flying in the sky. He does all of this while controlling a large motorcycle!

Travis has invented many tricks during his motocross career. In some tricks, Travis jumps into the air and controls his bike only with his legs. Travis can land smoothly without holding the handlebars! These tricks are extreme, daring, and dangerous. Travis had to practice a lot to be able to perform them safely. Travis is a pro, and he has to take safety seriously at every moment.

Travis flies through the air in the Superman seat grab trick at the 2003 Gravity Games, held in Cleveland, Ohio. Other motocross riders, and even BMX riders, enjoy doing this trick.

Travis stands on his seat and rides high to win a Gravity Games gold medal. Inset: Travis has injured his leg, ankles, back, and knees in motocross competitions. Travis was also hurt in a car accident in June 2003.

Safety First

Motocross is a very dangerous sport. Travis Pastrana has raced very successfully since he was a child, but he has often been slowed by **injuries**. He missed parts of the 2002 and 2003 seasons because of injuries. He is very skilled and safe, but sometimes that is not enough in motocross. If a person rides a 250-pound (113-kg) motorcycle 50 feet (15 m) into the air off a jump, things can go wrong if a trick is not performed perfectly. The AMA requires every rider to wear a helmet, sturdy gloves, and knee-high boots at every AMA event. A helmet **protects** the rider's head. Gloves and high boots made of sturdy leather or nylon protect the rider's arms and legs from flying rocks. Even wearing this protective clothing, Travis has been injured many times. If a professional like Travis can be injured so often, then safety should be every motocross rider's top **priority**.

Travis Pastrana's schoolwork is just as important in his life as motocross is. This is because Travis knows he will not race and do tricks on his motorcycle as a professional forever. After Travis is finished riding jumps, doing tricks, and racing, he will need another job.

Travis was **home-schooled** from sixth grade through twelfth grade. Travis even finished high school early! Travis goes to college in Maryland and is thinking about becoming a TV **broadcaster**. Though he is not certain what his next job will be, Travis will be ready because he will have a complete education. For now, look for Travis starring in motocross videos and racing his motorcycle at the X Games and other events. Maybe you will even see Travis perform a backflip, the most exciting trick in motocross!

Glossary

amateur (A-muh-tur) Someone who lacks practice in something.

broadcaster (BROD-kast-er) A person who gives facts and news on television.

champions (CHAM-pee-unz) The best, or the winners.

competition (kom-pih-TIH-shin) Game.

dangerous (DAYN-jer-us) Able to cause harm.

daredevil (DAYR-deh-vul) Extremely bold and daring.

difficult (DIH-fih-kult) Hard to do.

exciting (ik-SY-ting) Very interesting and fun.

extreme sport (ek-STREEM SPORT) An bold and uncommon sport, such as BMX, in-line skating, motocross, skateboarding, snowboarding, or wakeboarding.

home-schooled (HOHM-skoold) Taught at home instead of at school.

horizontal (hor-ih-ZON-til) Going from side to side.

injuries (IN-juh-reez) Physical harm done to a person.

medals (MEH-dulz) Small, round pieces of metal given as prizes.

obstacles (OB-stih-kulz) Objects that motocross riders use to perform tricks.

organized (OR-guh-nyzd) Arranged.

parallel (PAR-uh-lel) Being the same distance apart at all points.

perform (per-FORM) To carry out, to do.

priority (pry-OR-uh-tee) Something of great importance.

professionals (pruh-FEH-shuh-nulz) People who are paid for what they do.

protects (pruh-TEKTS) Keeps from harm.

ramp (RAMP) A sloping platform.

rookie (RU-kee) Referring to a player's first year.

sponsored (SPON-serd) Gave gear and money to a sportsman or sportswoman.

Index

A

AMA National Championship, 14

American Motorcycle Association (AMA), 14

B

big air, 13

C

competition, 9, 13, 17

E

engine(s), 6, 9

F

freeriding, 5, 13

freestyle, 13, 17

G

gears, 6

I

injuries, 21

L

Loretta Lynn's Amateur National Championships, 10

M

motocross, 5, 9–10, 14, 17–18, 21–22

motorcycle(s), 5–6, 9–10,14, 18, 21–22

N

National Amateur Championship, 10

P

Pastrana, Debby (mother), 6

Pastrana, Robert (father), 6, 9

R

racing, 5, 9

ramp, 17–18

Rookie of the Year, 14

S

safety, 9, 18

skateboarding, 5, 17

Southwick, 10

step up, 13

Superman seat grab, 18

Suzuki, 9

T

trick(s), 5, 10, 13, 18, 21–22

X

X Games, 17, 22

Web Sites

Due to the changing nature of Internet links, PowerKids Press has developed an online list of Web sites related to the subject of this book. This site is updated regularly. Please use this link to access the list: www.powerkidslinks.com/esb/pastrana/